KenKen For Kids!

By Sophie Kudler

To access free, unlimited puzzles of all sizes and difficulty levels, visit www.kenkenpuzzle.com.

Download the FREE KenKen Classic app for iOS and Android, available in the App Store and Google Play.

KenKen For Kids!

Puzzle contents copyright ©2021 KenKen Puzzle, LLC. All rights reserved.
KenKen is a registered trademark of KenKen Puzzle, LLC. All rights reserved.
www.kenkenpuzzle.com

Project editors: Tyler Kennedy, Jerry March
Designer: Tyler Kennedy
ISBN-13: 978-1-945542-10-7
First Edition: April 2021

Acknowledgements

I am so grateful for everyone who has helped me along this journey of writing my first book. First, I want to thank my father for introducing me to KenKen puzzles and helping to develop my passion for them. I not only have enjoyed our numerous hours of practicing, but also our informal competitions to determine who can solve a puzzle faster. I also extend my thanks to my mother and sister for supporting my KenKen endeavors. I want to express my appreciation to Robert Fuhrer, the President of KenKen Puzzle, LLC, for all of the opportunities to be involved with KenKen. Thanks so much to Tyler Kennedy for his many hours of hard work in designing and creating graphics for this book to help me achieve my vision for a children's book. Finally, I thank everyone at KenKen Puzzle LLC for publishing this book and for all of the guidance and mentorship.

Table of Contents

Chapter 1   Introducing LuLu and KenKen ——— 1

Chapter 2   Basic Terms and Rules ——————— 5

Chapter 3   How to Solve KenKens: The Steps — 15

Chapter 4   Solving 3x3 Puzzles ——————————— 19

Chapter 5   Solving 4x4 Puzzles ——————————— 46

Chapter 6   Solving 5x5 Puzzles ——————————— 78

Answers ———————————————————————— 104

Introducing LuLu!

Hi!

My name is LuLu! I'm LuLu the Kenguru! Being a KenKen guru means that I have mastered KenKen puzzles, and I want to help you become a guru, too!

Let's work together to master KenKen puzzles!

FUN FACT! The Japanese word "kangaeru" actually means "to think!"

What is KenKen?

KenKen is a number puzzle using
addition (+)
subtraction (−)
multiplication (x)
division (÷)
to fill in each box of the puzzle.

Here is a 3x3 puzzle using all 4 operations!

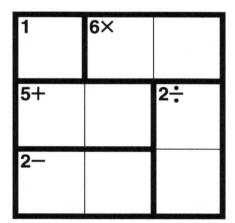

KenKen puzzles range in difficulty. You can solve puzzles as small as 3x3 and as large as 9x9.

Why KenKen?

KenKens are "Puzzles That Make You Smarter."© By learning how to solve KenKens, you will get better at addition, subtraction, multiplication, and division. You also will improve your problem-solving skills.

These skills will help you in all aspects of life!

The more you practice, the closer you'll be to mastering KenKen puzzles, arithmetic, problem-solving, and more!

The History of KenKen Puzzles

KenKen puzzles were invented in Japan by a teacher named Tetsuya Miyamoto, not a person named Ken!

Miyamoto created KenKen puzzles in 2004 to challenge elementary school students, like you, and teach them valuable lessons.

FUN FACT!
In Japanese, KenKen means "wisdom squared."

Basic Terms and Rules

Before we start solving some puzzles, it's important to go over the terms and rules!

After learning these terms and rules, you will have all the tools you need to master KenKens!

These rules will teach you the logic you need to solve KenKens without guessing! Again, there's no need to guess when solving a KenKen puzzle.

Feel free to come back to this chapter later if you want to refresh your memory on the rules and terms.

Now let's get started!

FUN FACT!
Every KenKen puzzle has exactly ONE solution!

Basic Terms

BOX:
one square in a puzzle

CAGE:
boxes outlined by a bold line

ROW:
a line of boxes from one side of the puzzle to the other side

COLUMN:
a line of boxes from the top of the puzzle to the bottom

Basic Terms

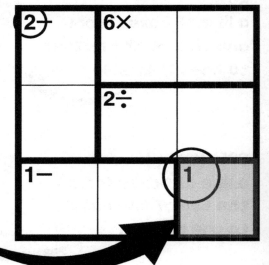

TARGET NUMBER: the number in the top left corner of each cage

FREEBIE: one bold box that only contains a target number

OPERATION:
the symbol next to the target number

NOTES:
small numbers written by you at the top of each box to show the numbers that could be written in the box

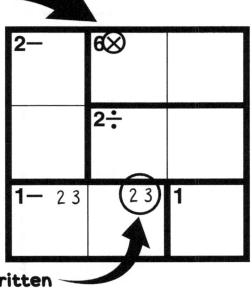

The +/−/x/÷ symbol tells you which operation is used to calculate the target number in that cage.

The Rules

1. **All KenKens are squares** with an equal number of rows and columns.

A 3x3 puzzle has 3 rows and 3 columns.

2. There are <u>no repeating numbers</u> in any row or column.

For example, a 3x3 puzzle only has the numbers 1 through 3 in each row and column.

3. The numbers in each cage combine to produce the target number.

For example, in a 3+ cage the two numbers add up to 3.

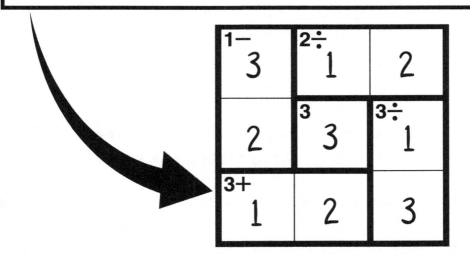

4. Order of numbers in a cage does not matter when you are writing notes.

For example, 3+ could be 1 and 2 or, depending on the puzzle, the order could be reversed to 2 and 1.

Coordinates for Rows and Columns

■ ▲ ●

	■	▲	●
A	5+ 2	3÷ 1	3
B	3	6× 2	1− 1
C	1 — 1	3	2

The shapes represent the columns.
The letters represent the rows.

Write the number from the puzzle above based on the shape and letter coordinates!
You'll see these coordinates throughout the book!

A■ = 2   B■ =   C■ =
A▲ =   B▲ =   C▲ =
A● =   B● =   C● =

	■	▲	●	◆
A	12× 3	2÷ 2	3− 1	4
B	1	4	3 3	6+ 2
C	4	1 1	2÷ 2	3
D	5+ 2	3	4	1

Now write the number for each coordinate from this puzzle!

A■ = ⬚   B■ = ⬚   C■ = ⬚   D■ = ⬚

A▲ = ⬚   B▲ = ⬚   C▲ = ⬚   D▲ = ⬚

A● = ⬚   B● = ⬚   C● = ⬚   D● = ⬚

A◆ = ⬚   B◆ = ⬚   C◆ = ⬚   D◆ = ⬚

How to Solve KenKens: The Steps

Step 1. <u>Write all possible numbers</u> for the rows and columns below the puzzle.

> Example: in a 3x3, write "1, 2, 3"
> Example: in a 4x4, write "1, 2, 3, 4"
> And so on...

5+	3÷	
	6×	1—
1		

(1 2 3)

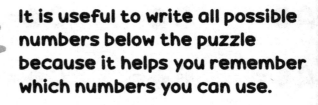

It is useful to write all possible numbers below the puzzle because it helps you remember which numbers you can use.

Step 2. Fill in any freebies.

5+	3÷	
	6×	1—
1 ①		

1 2 3

Step 3. A two-box locked cage occurs when only two numbers can be placed in the two boxes. Remember, the order of numbers in a locked cage does not matter when you are writing notes. The 3÷ cage below can be 1 and 3 or 3 and 1.
<u>Fill in the notes for the locked cages.</u>

For example, in a 3x3 puzzle, 6x is a locked cage because only 2x3=6.

5+ 2 3	3÷ 1 3	1 3
2 3	6× 2 3	1−
1 1	2 3	

1 2 3

1− is not a locked cage because 3−2=1 and 2−1=1

FUN FACT!
In larger puzzles (up to 9x9), you may find larger locked cages with three or four boxes (or more)!

Step 4. <u>Fill in the remaining cages,</u> staying aware of the locked cages while not repeating a number in any row or column.

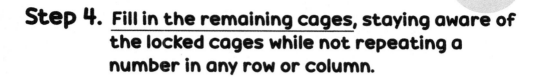

1 2 3

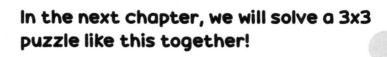

In the next chapter, we will solve a 3x3 puzzle like this together!

18

Solving 3x3 Puzzles

Now, let's start solving KenKens! We're going to start with 3x3 puzzles, which are the smallest KenKens.

We'll solve two puzzles together, and then you can practice on your own.

Let's master 3x3 puzzles!

FUN FACT!
Each row and column of a 3x3 puzzle adds to equal 6 (1+2+3=6)!

Here's an addition-only 3x3 puzzle. Let's get started!

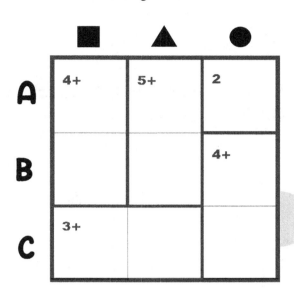

Step 1. <u>Write all possible numbers.</u> Write the numbers 1, 2, and 3 below the puzzle.

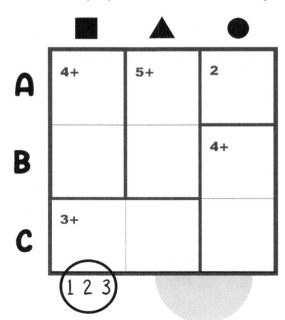

20

Step 2. Fill in any freebies. In this puzzle, the only freebie is a 2 at A.

	■	▲	●
A	4+	5+	2 → 2
B			4+
C	3+		

1 2 3

Step 3. Fill in the notes for the locked cages. In this puzzle, all of the cages are locked cages!

	■	▲	●
A	4+ 1 3	5+ 2 3	2 *2*
B	1 3	2 3	4+ 1 3
C	3+ 1 2	1 2	1 3

1 2 3

22

Step 4. Fill in the remaining cages. Solve the puzzle using the freebie and the notes in the locked cages.

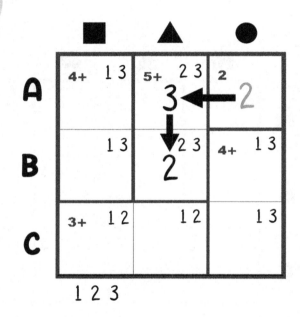

Because A● is 2, A▲ must be 3 because there can only be one 2 in row A. If A▲ is 3, then B▲ is 2 because 3+2=5.

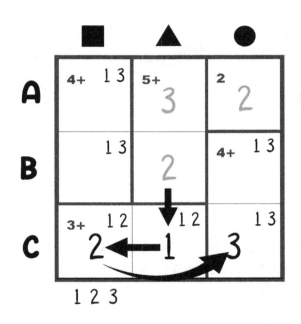

Now we can finish column ▲. C▲ has to be 1 because it is the only number missing in column ▲. If C▲ is 1, then C■ is 2. Then we can finish row C by filling in 3 for C●.

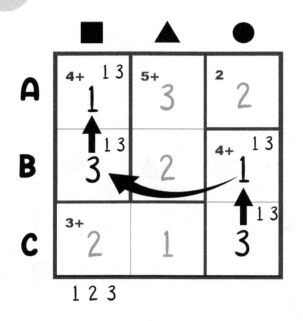

If C● is 3, then B● is 1. Now, we can complete row B. The only number missing in row B is 3, so B■ is 3. If B■ is 3, then A■ is 1.

Kengratulations, we finished the puzzle!

Now that we've solved an addition–only puzzle, let's solve an all-operation puzzle together!

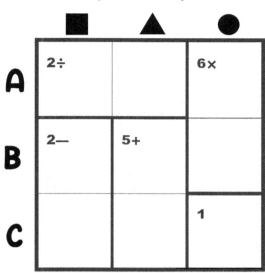

Step 1. Write all possible numbers. Write the numbers 1, 2, and 3 below the puzzle.

Step 2. Fill in any freebies. In this puzzle, the only freebie is a 1 at C●.

Step 3. Fill in the notes for the locked cages. In this puzzle, all of the two-box cages are locked cages!

	■	▲	●
A	2÷ 1 2	1 2	6× 2 3
B	2− 1 3	5+ 2 3	2 3
C	1 3	2 3	1 *1*

1 2 3

Step 4. Fill in the remaining cages. Solve the puzzle using the freebie and the notes in the locked cages.

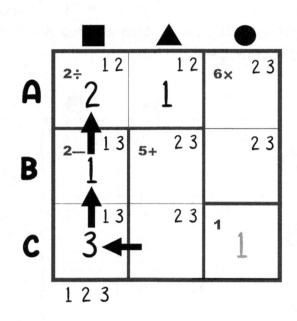

Because C● is 1, there can't be a 1 anywhere else in row C, so C■ is 3. B■ must be 1 because 3−1=2. Now, the only number left in column ■ is 2, so A■ is 2. A▲ must be 1 because 2÷1=2.

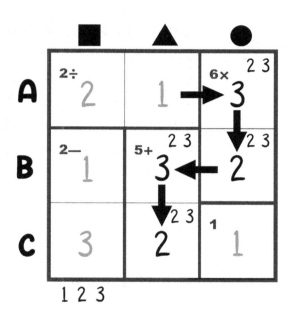

The only number remaining in the top row is 3, so A● is 3. That means B● is 2 because 2×3=6. Now, the only cage left is 5+. We know that B▲ must be 3 to complete row B, and C▲ must be 2 because 3+2=5.

Kengratulations, we completed the puzzle!

Now, you are ready to solve 3x3 puzzles on your own! Don't worry, I am here to give you helpful hints along the way! Keep an eye out for LuLu Lessons at the bottom of some pages to help you solve the puzzle.

Let's get started!

The answers to the puzzles in this chapter start on page 105.

FUN FACT!
On average, 3 million KenKen puzzles are played every month on the official KenKen website, www.kenkenpuzzle.com!

Addition-only 3x3 Puzzles

Puzzle #1

3+	7+	
	2	
3	3+	

Puzzle #2

5+		4+
3+		
3	3+	

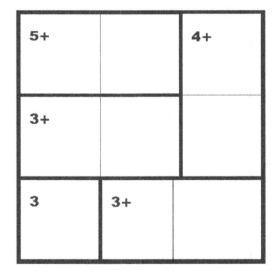

LuLu Lesson: Remember, in any puzzle, 3+ is a locked cage because only 1+2=3.

Puzzle #3

2	3+	4+
4+		
	5+	

Puzzle #4

4+	5+	2
		4+
3+		

LuLu Lesson:
In any puzzle, 4+ is a locked cage because 1 and 3 are the only numbers that can add to 4 (2+2 is not allowed under the rules).

Puzzle #5

5+		3+
4+	1	
	5+	

Puzzle #6

5+	3+	1
		5+
4+		

LuLu Lesson:
In a 3x3 puzzle, 5+ in two boxes is a locked cage because only 2+3=5. As a general rule, the sum of the two largest numbers in the puzzle is a locked cage. 2 and 3 are the two largest numbers in a 3x3 puzzle.

Puzzle #7

4+		7+
3+		
	4+	

Puzzle #8

3+	5+	
	6+	
4+		

LuLu Lesson:
Some puzzles do not have any freebies. If there aren't any freebies, begin with Step 2 by filling in all of the locked cages' notes.

Addition/Subtraction 3x3 Puzzles

Puzzle #9

2−		1−
5+		
2	2−	

Puzzle #10

5+		2−
1−	2−	
		2

LuLu Lesson:
In a 3x3 puzzle, 2− is a locked cage because only 3−1=2. As a general rule, the largest number in the puzzle minus 1 is a locked cage.

Puzzle #11

8+	1	1−
1−		3

Puzzle #12

1−		1−
2−		
1	5+	

LuLu Lesson:
In any puzzle, save 1− cages for later because there are too many options for each box. In a 3x3 puzzle it could be 3-2 or 2-1, and in larger puzzles there are even more options.

Multiplication/Division 3x3 Puzzles

Puzzle #13

6×	3×	
		6×
2÷		

Puzzle #14

3÷	6×	1
		6×
2×		

LuLu Lesson:
In a 3x3 puzzle, 6x in two boxes is a locked cage because only 2x3=6.

Puzzle #15

2÷	2	9×
3	2÷	

Puzzle #16

2÷		6×
3÷		
2	3×	

All-Operation 3x3 Puzzles

Puzzle #17

3÷	12×	
	1	
2	2—	

Puzzle #18

3+	1—	
	1—	3÷
3		

Puzzle #19

1—	3×	
		5+
2÷		

Puzzle #20

5+		6×
1		
2÷		3

41

Puzzle #21

2÷	3÷	
	12×	
3÷		

Puzzle #22

5+		1—
3÷		
2	3÷	

LuLu Lesson:
In a 3x3 puzzle, 3÷ is a locked cage because only 3÷1=3.

Puzzle #23

6×	3÷	2
		2—
1—		

Puzzle #24

2—		1—
6×	2÷	
		1

43

Puzzle #25

2−		2
2÷	1−	
	3÷	

45

Sell your books at
sellbackyourBook.com!
Go to sellbackyourBook.com
and get an instant price
quote. We even pay the
shipping - see what your old
books are worth today!

Inspected By:

Sell your books at
sellbackyourBook.com!
Go to sellbackyourBook.com
and get an instant price
quote. We even pay the
shipping - see what your old
books are worth today!

Inspected By:

KENKEN®
www.kenkenpuzzle.com
Puzzles That Make You Smarter ©

has mastered

3x3 Puzzles

Kengratulations!

Signed: _LuLu_ Date: _____

Solving 4x4 Puzzles

Now that you've mastered 3x3 puzzles, it is time to solve 4x4 puzzles! 4x4 puzzles are solved using the same steps as 3x3 puzzles, so you already know what to do!

4x4 puzzles are larger than 3x3 puzzles, which means they are a little more difficult. Don't worry, we'll solve the first two puzzles together, and then you can practice on your own!

Let's master 4x4 puzzles!

FUN FACT!
Each row and column of a 4x4 puzzle adds to 1o (1+2+3+4=1o)!

Here's an addition-only 4x4 puzzle. Let's get started!

	■	▲	●	◆
A	4	4+	7+	
B	3+		7+	
C		4		5+
D	6+			

Step 1. <u>Write all possible numbers.</u> Write the numbers 1, 2, 3, and 4 below the puzzle.

	■	▲	●	◆
A	4	4+	7+	
B	3+		7+	
C		4		5+
D	6+			

1 2 3 4

Step 2. Fill in any freebies. In this puzzle, there are two freebies: 4 at A■ and 4 at C▲.

	■	▲	●	◆
A	⁴ 4	4+	7+	
B	3+		7+	
C		⁴ 4		5+
D	6+			

1 2 3 4

48

Step 3. Fill in the notes for the locked cages. As you can see, there are four locked cages, and the notes are filled in below.

	■	▲	●	◆
A	⁴ 4	4+ ¹³	7+	
B	3+ ¹²	¹³	7+ ³⁴	
C	¹²	⁴ 4	³⁴	5+
D	6+ ¹²³	¹²³	¹²³	

1 2 3 4

Step 4. <u>Fill in the remaining cages.</u> Solve the puzzle using the freebie and the notes in the locked cages.

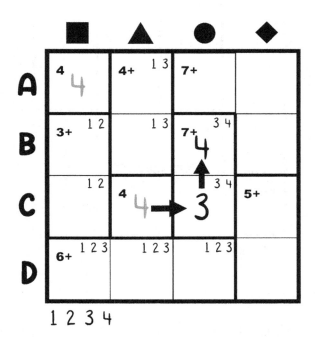

Because we know C▲ is 4, that means C● has to be 3. If C● is 3, then B● is 4 because 3+4=7.

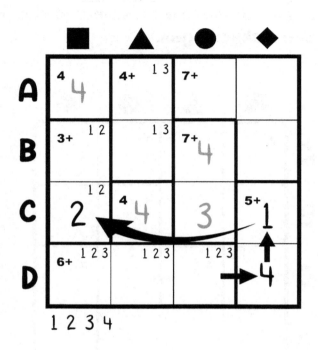

Now, let's look at row D. If we know that the 6+ cage must include 1, 2, and 3, then the only place for 4 in row D is D◆. If D◆ is 4, then C◆ is 1 because 4+1=5. Now, we can finish row C. C■ has to be 2.

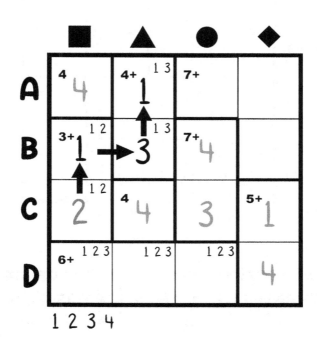

If C■ is 2, then B■ is 1 because 2+1=3. If B■ is 1, then B▲ is 3. Then, A▲ is 1 because 3+1=4.

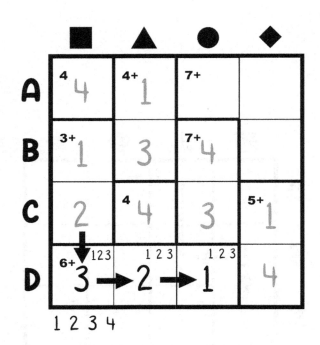

Now, we can continue by completing column ■ so it has the numbers 1, 2, 3, and 4. D■ has to be 3, and D▲ has to be 2. If D■ is 3 and D▲ is 2, then D● is 1.

LuLu Lesson:
Save cages with many options, like the 7+ cage, for later because it will be easier to reduce the options for each box of the cage when most of the other boxes are filled.

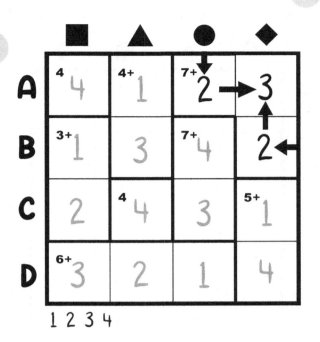

We are almost done! Instead of figuring out all of the different ways to add to 7, let's just complete the rows and columns until the puzzle is done! A● has to be 2 to complete column ●, and B◆ has to be 2 to complete row B. Finally, A◆ has to be 3, and the math works out because 2+3+2=7!

Kengratulations, we completed the puzzle!

54

Now that we've solved an addition-only puzzle, let's solve an all-operation puzzle together!

	■	▲	●	◆
A	6×		9+	
B	2÷	1−		
C		3−		1−
D	4	4+		

- - - - - - - - - - - - - - - - - - -

Step 1. <u>Write all possible numbers.</u> Write the numbers 1, 2, 3, and 4 below the puzzle.

	■	▲	●	◆
A	6×		9+	
B	2÷	1−		
C		3−		1−
D	4	4+		

1 2 3 4

Step 2. Fill in any freebies. In this puzzle, the only freebie is a 4 in D■.

	■	▲	●	◆
A	6×		9+	
B	2÷	1−		
C		3−		1−
D	⁴ 4	4+		

1 2 3 4

Step 3. Fill in the notes for the locked cages. As you can see, there are three locked cages, and the notes are filled in below.

	■	▲	●	◆
A	6× 2 3	2 3	9+	
B	2÷	1—		
C		3— 1 4	1 4	1—
D	4 4	4+ 1 3	1 3	

1 2 3 4

57

Step 4. <u>Fill in the remaining cages.</u> Solve the puzzle using the freebie and the notes in the locked cages.

	■	▲	●	◆
A	6× ²³	²³	9+	
B	2÷	1—		
C		3— ¹⁴	¹⁴	1— ¹³ **3**
D	⁴ **4**	4+ ¹³	¹³	**2**

1 2 3 4

Let's start with row D. Every row and column has to have 1, 2, 3, and 4, and 1, 3, and 4 already are filled in with numbers or notes, so D◆ is 2. If there is a 2 in a 1— cage, the only options for C◆ are 1 and 3 because 3−2=1 and 2−1=1. There already is a 1 in the notes of the locked cage in row C, so C◆ is 3.

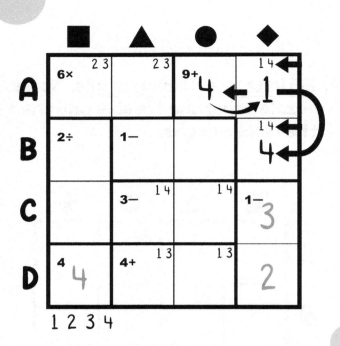

Now let's fill in the notes for column ◆. Only 1 and 4 are missing, so let's put 1 and 4 in the notes for A◆ and B◆. We know the boxes in that three-box cage add up to 9, and we know A◆ and B◆ are 1 and 4. So, 1+4=5, and 9−5=4, so A● is 4. Because A● is 4, A◆ must be 1, and B◆ must be 4. The math works because 4+1+4=9.

LuLu Lesson:
You can't have the same number twice in a row or column, but you can have the same number twice in a cage if the numbers follow the rules, like the 9+ cage in this puzzle.

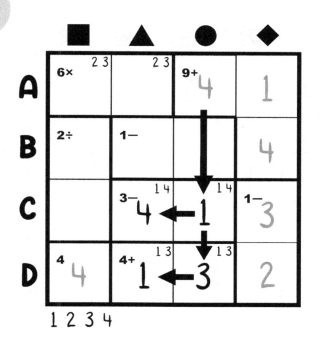

Looking at column ●, there is a 4 in row A, so there are no other 4s in column ●, so C● is 1. If C● is 1, C▲ is 4. Looking at column ● again, if C● is 1, D● must be 3. If D● is 3, D▲ must be 1.

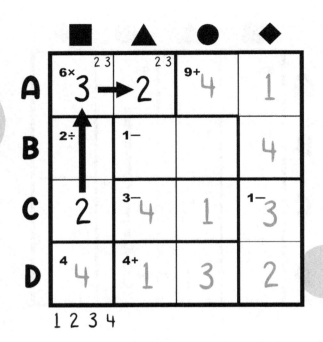

To finish row C, the only number missing is 2, so C■ is 2. Looking at column ■, if C■ is 2, A■ must be 3. If A■ is 3, then A▲ must be 2.

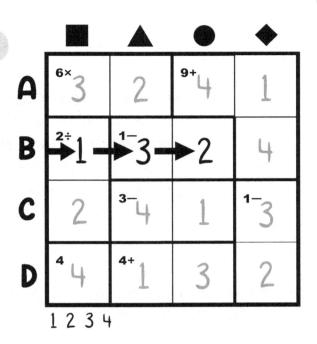

Now, we will complete the puzzle by finishing each column. In column ■, only a 1 is missing, so B■ is 1. That math works out because 2÷1=2. In column ▲, only a 3 is missing, so B▲ is 3. In column ●, only a 2 is missing, so B● is 2. That math also works because 3−2=1.

Kengratulations, we completed the puzzle!

Now, you are ready to solve 4x4 puzzles on your own! Remember to look for LuLu Lessons at the bottom of some pages to help you solve the puzzles.

There is one new vocabulary word I will be using in my LuLu Lessons – a snake.

A snake is a three-box locked cage with all boxes lined up in the same direction (called that because it looks like a snake).

Let's get started!

The answers to the puzzles in this chapter start on page 109.

FUN FACT!
KenKen puzzles are played in over 150 countries.

Addition-only 4x4 Puzzles

Puzzle #26

8+	6+		3+
	7+		
		6+	
6+		4+	

Puzzle #27

6+	4+	5+	
		3	7+
8+			
	6+		1

LuLu Lesson:
In a 4x4 puzzle, 6+ in two boxes is a locked cage because only 2+4=6 (3+3 is not allowed under the rules).

64

Puzzle #28

7+	7+		5+
	1		
7+	7+		2
		4+	

Puzzle #29

3+	7+		1
	5+		7+
7+	3+		
	1	6+	

LuLu Lesson:
In a 4x4 puzzle, 7+ in two boxes is a locked cage because only 3+4=7. This follows the general rule: the sum of the two largest numbers in the puzzle is a locked cage. 3 and 4 are the two largest numbers in a 4x4 puzzle.

Puzzle #30

6+			13+
3	7+		
5+			
6+			

Puzzle #31

7+		8+	3+
3+			
	10+		4
		5+	

LuLu Lesson:
In any puzzle, save large cages for later, like the 13+ cage in puzzle #30, and the 10+ cage in puzzle #31.

Puzzle #32

4	4+	7+	
3+		7+	
	4		5+
6+			

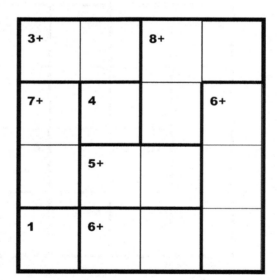

Puzzle #33

3+		8+	
7+	4		6+
	5+		
1	6+		

LuLu Lesson:
In any puzzle, 6+ in three boxes going in the same direction is a locked cage because only 1+2+3=6. The 6+ cages with three boxes in the puzzles above are snakes.

Addition/Subtraction 4x4 Puzzles

Puzzle #34

4+	1−		2−
	3−		
2−	3+	8+	
		3	

Puzzle #35

1−	3+		7+
	4	6+	
3−			3+
	7+		

Puzzle #36

1−	3	3−	
	3−	5+	1−
5+			
	2−		3

Puzzle #37

8+		3−	
3+		2−	
	3−		5+
5+		3	

> **LuLu Lesson:**
> In a 4x4 puzzle, 3− is a locked cage because only 4−1=3. This follows the general rule: the largest number in the puzzle minus 1 is a locked cage.

Multiplication/Division 4x4 Puzzles

Puzzle #38

2÷	12×		4
	12×		2÷
12×		6×	
	2		

Puzzle #39

12×		6×	2÷
12×			
	2÷	4×	12×
2			

LuLu Lesson:
In a 4x4 puzzle, 12x in two boxes is a locked cage because only 3x4=12.

70

Puzzle #40

2÷	24×		
	12×	2÷	4
12×			2÷
		3	

Puzzle #41

12×		2÷	
24×		8×	
	2÷		3
		3×	

LuLu Lesson:
In a 4x4 puzzle, 24x is a snake because it is a locked cage with three boxes lined up in the same direction, and only 2x3x4=24.

All-Operation 4x4 Puzzles

Puzzle #42

1−	2÷	5+	
		6×	
2÷	1−	2÷	
			3

Puzzle #43

2÷	12×		8+
	2÷		
1−		2	2÷
	2−		

LuLu Lesson:
In a 4x4 puzzle, the only options for 2÷ are 4, 2, and 1. This is not a locked cage, but it is important to remember that one of the boxes in the cage MUST be a 2 because the only options for 2÷ are 4÷2=2 and 2÷1=2.

Puzzle #44

3+	12×		2
	3−	7+	
3		2÷	4+
2÷			

Puzzle #45

7+		3−	6×
3+	2		
	4+	1−	
4		2÷	

Puzzle #46

2	7+		4+
3−		6×	
7+	1		2÷
	3+		

Puzzle #47

12×	5+	2	3−
		3−	
2÷			3
5+		6×	

Puzzle #48

2÷		36×	
1−	5+	2−	
			1−
1−		1	

Puzzle #49

3−	6×		1
	7+		2−
1−	2÷		
	1	1−	

LuLu Lesson:
Remember, save 1− cages for later because there are so many options.

Puzzle #50

12×	3	3+	2÷
2÷	3−		2−
	1−		

KENKEN®
www.kenkenpuzzle.com
Puzzles That Make You Smarter ©

_____ has mastered

4x4 Puzzles

Kengratulations!

Signed: _LuLu_   Date: _____

Solving 5x5 Puzzles

Now, you are ready to solve 5x5 puzzles! As the puzzle size increases, the difficulty increases.

You solve 5x5 puzzles the same way you solve 3x3 and 4x4 puzzles, so I'm going to let you dive right into 5x5 puzzles without doing one together.

Here is something important to remember when solving 5x5 puzzles:

In a 5x5 puzzle, any multiplication cage with a target number ending in 0 or 5 MUST have the number 5 in that cage.

Remember, LuLu Lessons are at the bottom of some pages to give you tips to solve the puzzles.

FUN FACT!
30,000 teachers across the world use KenKen Classroom. It's a weekly puzzle set of various KenKens and fun brain teasers sent throughout the school year. Find out more at kenken.com/teachers/classroom.

Addition-only 5x5 Puzzles

Puzzle #51

6+		8+	6+	
5+			4+	9+
6+	3+			
	3	9+		4+
9+		3+		

LuLu Lesson:
In a 5x5 puzzle, 9+ in two boxes is a locked cage because only the numbers 4 and 5 are in the notes. This follows the general rule: the sum of the two largest numbers in the puzzle is a locked cage. 4 and 5 are the two largest numbers in a 5x5 puzzle.

Puzzle #52

3+		12+		
9+		9+		
1	5+	10+		
7+			3+	7+
	9+			

Puzzle #53

4+		7+	3+	10+
9+				
3+		9+		
5	3+		13+	
9+				

LuLu Lesson:
Remember, 3+ is a locked cage in every puzzle because only 1+2=3.

Puzzle #54

3+		7+		8+
10+	3+		9+	
		5		
9+		5+		3+
7+		6+		

Puzzle #55

4+		7+		4
6+	9+	3+	8+	
			13+	
3+		10+		
8+				

Puzzle #56

9+		3+		8+
3+		8+	7+	
7+				
6+	9+		8+	
		7+		

LuLu Lesson:
In a 5x5 puzzle, 8+ in two boxes is a locked cage because only 3 and 5 can add to 8 (4+4 is not allowed under the rules).

Puzzle #57

4+		6+		8+
5	3+		9+	
3+	9+	5+		5+
			3	
7+		6+		2

Puzzle #58

9+		9+		6+
3		3+		
3+		7+		6+
9+		10+		
6+			4+	

Addition/Subtraction 5x5 Puzzles

Puzzle #59

1	9+		1−	
9+		7+	4−	3+
8+	2			
	3+		7+	
5+		3−		5

Puzzle #60

9+		3+		3
3+		7+	5	5+
2	4−		7+	
7+		2		3−
	3	4−		

Puzzle #61

5+	4+		4−	6+
	13+			
9+	3		5+	4−
	3+			
4−		9+		

LuLu Lesson:
In a 5x5 puzzle, 4− is a locked cage because only 5−1=4. This follows the general rule: the largest number in the puzzle minus 1 is a locked cage.

Puzzle #62

9+		10+	8+	
5+			4−	
3−	4−			10+
		4	6+	
3	3+			

Multiplication/Division 5x5 Puzzles

Puzzle #63

5×		2÷		3×
4×	10×		15×	
	2÷	15×		4
6×			2÷	
	3×		20×	

LuLu Lesson:
In every puzzle, 15x in two boxes is a locked cage because only 3x5=15. Remember to keep an eye out for multiplication involving fives!

Puzzle #64

12×	2÷		40×	15×
	1			
	15×		2÷	
30×	2÷		12×	
		20×		

Puzzle #65

1	18×	2÷	5×	20×
2÷	25×	3	12×	2÷
20×		2÷		3

Puzzle #66

15×		2÷		20×
	15×	6×		
2÷		20×		3×
	2÷			
1		30×		

All-Operation 5x5 Puzzles

Puzzle #67

6×		4−		9+
4+		2÷	2	
9+	3−		6×	
		2−		
2	4−		7+	

95

Puzzle #68

5	6×		9+	
1−	4−		2	
	2÷	8+	4−	
2÷			5+	
	3−		15×	

Puzzle #69

4+		4−	2÷	
2÷			75×	
3	6+	2÷		
11+		1−	4+	
			5+	

LuLu Lesson:
Look out for cages using multiplication with multiples of 25. 5x5=25, which means that two fives must be in that cage. For example, 75=5x5x3.

Puzzle #70

12×		8+		
2÷	4−	1−	2÷	
			75×	
2−	2−	2÷		4
			4+	

Puzzle #71

4−	2−	10×	12×	
				3
3+		3	1−	
3	20×		10×	2÷
12×				

LuLu Lesson:
In every puzzle, 10x in two boxes is a locked cage because only 2x5=10.

Puzzle #72

2÷		2−	10×	9+
3−	3			
	2÷	1−		4+
5		24×		
8+			2÷	

Puzzle #73

4−		6×		2÷
12×		9+	4−	
3+	2			8+
	20×	4+		
3			3−	

Puzzle #74

1−	2÷		10×	4
	5			1−
4−	2÷	15×	7+	
				6+
1−		5+		

Puzzle #75

12×	10×		15×	
	9+	2÷	2÷	
2÷				12+
	3	2−		
4−			2÷	

103

KENKEN®
www.kenkenpuzzle.com
Puzzles That Make You Smarter ©

has mastered
5x5 Puzzles

Kengratulations!

Signed: _LuLu_   Date: _____

Answers

Puzzle #1

³⁺2	⁷⁺3	1
1	²2	3
³3	³⁺1	2

Puzzle #2

⁵⁺2	3	⁴⁺1
³⁺1	2	3
³3	³⁺1	2

Puzzle #3

²2	³⁺1	⁴⁺3
⁴⁺3	2	1
1	⁵⁺3	2

Puzzle #4

⁴⁺1	⁵⁺3	²2
3	2	⁴⁺1
³⁺2	1	3

Puzzle #5

⁵⁺2	3	³⁺1
⁴⁺3	¹1	2
1	⁵⁺2	3

Puzzle #6

⁵⁺3	³⁺2	¹1
2	1	⁵⁺3
⁴⁺1	3	2

105

Puzzle #7

$^{4+}$3	1	$^{7+}$2
$^{3+}$1	2	3
2	$^{4+}$3	1

Puzzle #8

$^{3+}$1	$^{5+}$2	3
2	$^{6+}$3	1
$^{4+}$3	1	2

Puzzle #9

$^{2-}$1	3	$^{1-}$2
$^{5+}$3	2	1
^{2}2	$^{2-}$1	3

Puzzle #10

$^{5+}$3	2	$^{2-}$1
$^{1-}$2	$^{2-}$1	3
1	3	^{2}2

Puzzle #11

$^{8+}$3	^{1}1	$^{1-}$2
2	3	1
$^{1-}$1	2	^{3}3

Puzzle #12

$^{1-}$2	3	$^{1-}$1
$^{2-}$3	1	2
^{1}1	$^{5+}$2	3

Puzzle #13

$^{6\times}$2	$^{3\times}$3	1
3	1	$^{6\times}$2
$^{2\div}$1	2	3

Puzzle #14

$^{3\div}$3	$^{6\times}$2	^{1}1
1	3	$^{6\times}$2
$^{2\times}$2	1	3

Puzzle #15

$^{2\div}$1	^{2}2	$^{9\times}$3
2	3	1
^{3}3	$^{2\div}$1	2

Puzzle #16

$^{2\div}$1	2	$^{6\times}$3
$^{3\div}$3	1	2
^{2}2	$^{3\times}$3	1

Puzzle #17

$^{3\div}$1	$^{12\times}$2	3
3	^{1}1	2
^{2}2	$^{2-}$3	1

Puzzle #18

$^{3+}$1	$^{1-}$3	2
2	$^{1-}$1	$^{3\div}$3
^{3}3	2	1

Puzzle #19

$^{1-}2$	$^{3\times}3$	1
3	1	$^{5+}2$
$^{2\div}1$	2	3

Puzzle #20

$^{5+}3$	2	$^{6\times}1$
$^{1}1$	3	2
$^{2\div}2$	1	$^{3}3$

Puzzle #21

$^{2\div}2$	$^{3\div}3$	1
1	$^{12\times}2$	3
$^{3\div}3$	1	2

Puzzle #22

$^{5+}3$	2	$^{1-}1$
$^{3\div}1$	3	2
$^{2}2$	$^{3\div}1$	3

Puzzle #23

$^{6\times}3$	$^{3\div}1$	$^{2}2$
2	3	$^{2-}1$
$^{1-}1$	2	3

Puzzle #24

$^{2-}1$	3	$^{1-}2$
$^{6\times}2$	$^{2\div}1$	3
3	2	$^{1}1$

108

Puzzle #25

$2-$ 3	1	2 2	
$2\div$ 1	$1-$ 2	3	
2	$3\div$ 3	1	

Puzzle #26

$8+$ 3	$6+$ 2	4	$3+$ 1
4	$7+$ 1	3	2
1	3	$6+$ 2	4
$6+$ 2	4	$4+$ 1	3

Puzzle #27

$6+$ 2	$4+$ 3	$5+$ 1	4
4	1	3 3	$7+$ 2
$8+$ 1	4	2	3
3	$6+$ 2	4	1 1

Puzzle #28

$7+$ 4	$7+$ 2	3	$5+$ 1
3	1 1	2	4
$7+$ 1	$7+$ 3	4	2 2
2	4	$4+$ 1	3

Puzzle #29

$3+$ 2	$7+$ 4	3	1 1
1	$5+$ 3	2	$7+$ 4
$7+$ 4	$3+$ 2	1	3
3	1 1	$6+$ 4	2

Puzzle #30

$6+$ 2	3	1	$13+$ 4
3 3	$7+$ 1	4	2
$5+$ 1	4	2	3
$6+$ 4	2	3	1

109

Puzzle #31

$^{7+}$3	4	$^{8+}$1	$^{3+}$2
$^{3+}$2	3	4	1
1	$^{10+}$2	3	^{4}4
4	1	$^{5+}$2	3

Puzzle #32

^{4}4	$^{4+}$1	$^{7+}$2	3
$^{3+}$1	3	$^{7+}$4	2
2	^{4}4	3	$^{5+}$1
$^{6+}$3	2	1	4

Puzzle #33

$^{3+}$2	1	$^{8+}$3	4
$^{7+}$3	^{4}4	1	$^{6+}$2
4	$^{5+}$3	2	1
^{1}1	$^{6+}$2	4	3

Puzzle #34

$^{4+}$1	$^{1-}$3	2	$^{2-}$4
3	$^{3-}$4	1	2
$^{2-}$2	$^{3+}$1	$^{8+}$4	3
4	2	^{3}3	1

Puzzle #35

$^{1-}$3	$^{3+}$1	2	$^{7+}$4
2	^{4}4	$^{6+}$1	3
$^{3-}$4	2	3	$^{3+}$1
1	$^{7+}$3	4	2

Puzzle #36

$^{1-}$2	^{3}3	$^{3-}$1	4
3	$^{3-}$4	$^{5+}$2	$^{1-}$1
$^{5+}$4	1	3	2
1	$^{2-}$2	4	^{3}3

Puzzle #37

$^{8+}$3	2	$^{3-}$4	1
$^{3+}$1	3	$^{2-}$2	4
2	$^{3-}$4	1	$^{5+}$3
$^{5+}$4	1	^{3}3	2

Puzzle #38

$^{2\div}$2	$^{12\times}$1	3	^{4}4
1	$^{12\times}$3	4	$^{2\div}$2
$^{12\times}$3	4	$^{6\times}$2	1
4	^{2}2	1	3

Puzzle #39

$^{12\times}$1	4	$^{6\times}$3	$^{2\div}$2
$^{12\times}$4	3	2	1
3	$^{2\div}$2	$^{4\times}$1	$^{12\times}$4
^{2}2	1	4	3

Puzzle #40

$^{2\div}$1	$^{24\times}$2	4	3
2	$^{12\times}$3	$^{2\div}$1	^{4}4
$^{12\times}$3	4	2	$^{2\div}$1
4	1	^{3}3	2

Puzzle #41

$^{12\times}$1	3	$^{2\div}$2	4
$^{24\times}$3	4	$^{8\times}$1	2
2	$^{2\div}$1	4	^{3}3
4	2	$^{3\times}$3	1

Puzzle #42

$^{1-}$3	$^{2\div}$2	$^{5+}$1	4
4	1	$^{6\times}$3	2
$^{2\div}$2	$^{1-}$3	$^{2\div}$4	1
1	4	2	^{3}3

Puzzle #43

$^{2\div}$2	$^{12\times}$4	3	$^{8+}$1
1	$^{2\div}$2	4	3
$^{1-}$3	1	^{2}2	$^{2\div}$4
4	$^{2-}$3	1	2

Puzzle #44

$^{3+}$1	$^{12\times}$3	4	^{2}2
2	$^{3-}$1	$^{7+}$3	4
^{3}3	4	$^{2\div}$2	$^{4+}$1
$^{2\div}$4	2	1	3

Puzzle #45

$^{7+}$3	4	$^{3-}$1	$^{6\times}$2
$^{3+}$1	^{2}2	4	3
2	$^{4+}$1	$^{1-}$3	4
^{4}4	3	$^{2\div}$2	1

Puzzle #46

^{2}2	$^{7+}$3	4	$^{4+}$1
$^{3-}$1	4	$^{6\times}$2	3
$^{7+}$4	^{1}1	3	$^{2\div}$2
3	$^{3+}$2	1	4

Puzzle #47

$^{12\times}$4	$^{5+}$3	^{2}2	$^{3-}$1
3	2	$^{3-}$1	4
$^{2\div}$2	1	4	^{3}3
$^{5+}$1	4	$^{6\times}$3	2

Puzzle #48

$^{2\div}$1	2	$^{36\times}$3	4
$^{1-}$2	$^{5+}$1	$^{2-}$4	3
3	4	2	$^{1-}$1
$^{1-}$4	3	^{1}1	2

112

Puzzle #49

$^{3-}$4	$^{6\times}$3	2	^{1}1
1	$^{7+}$4	3	$^{2-}$2
$^{1-}$3	$^{2\div}$2	1	4
2	^{1}1	$^{1-}$4	3

Puzzle #50

$^{12\times}$1	^{3}3	$^{3+}$2	$^{2\div}$4
3	4	1	2
$^{2\div}$2	$^{3-}$1	4	$^{2-}$3
4	$^{1-}$2	3	1

Puzzle #51

$^{6+}$1	5	$^{8+}$3	$^{6+}$4	2
$^{5+}$3	2	5	$^{4+}$1	$^{9+}$4
$^{6+}$4	$^{3+}$1	2	3	5
2	^{3}3	$^{9+}$4	5	$^{4+}$1
$^{9+}$5	4	$^{3+}$1	2	3

Puzzle #52

$^{3+}$2	1	$^{12+}$3	5	4
$^{9+}$5	4	$^{9+}$2	3	1
^{1}1	$^{5+}$2	$^{10+}$5	4	3
$^{7+}$4	3	1	$^{3+}$2	$^{7+}$5
3	$^{9+}$5	4	1	2

Puzzle #53

$^{4+}$1	3	$^{7+}$4	$^{3+}$2	$^{10+}$5
$^{9+}$4	5	3	1	2
$^{3+}$2	1	$^{9+}$5	4	3
^{5}5	$^{3+}$2	1	$^{13+}$3	4
$^{9+}$3	4	2	5	1

Puzzle #54

$^{3+}$1	2	$^{7+}$4	3	$^{8+}$5
$^{10+}$5	$^{3+}$1	2	$^{9+}$4	3
2	3	^{5}5	1	4
$^{9+}$4	5	$^{5+}$3	2	$^{3+}$1
$^{7+}$3	4	$^{6+}$1	5	2

Puzzle #55

⁴⁺3	1	⁷⁺5	2	⁴4
⁶⁺2	⁹⁺4	³⁺1	⁸⁺5	3
4	5	2	¹³⁺3	1
³⁺1	2	¹⁰⁺3	4	5
⁸⁺5	3	4	1	2

Puzzle #56

⁹⁺5	4	³⁺1	2	⁸⁺3
³⁺1	2	⁸⁺3	⁷⁺4	5
⁷⁺4	3	5	1	2
⁶⁺2	⁹⁺5	4	⁸⁺3	1
3	1	⁷⁺2	5	4

Puzzle #57

⁴⁺3	1	⁶⁺4	2	⁸⁺5
⁵5	³⁺2	1	⁹⁺4	3
³⁺2	⁹⁺4	⁵⁺3	5	⁵⁺1
1	5	2	³3	4
⁷⁺4	3	⁶⁺5	1	²2

Puzzle #58

⁹⁺1	3	⁹⁺4	5	⁶⁺2
³3	5	³⁺1	2	4
³⁺2	1	⁷⁺3	4	⁶⁺5
⁹⁺5	4	¹⁰⁺2	3	1
⁶⁺4	2	5	⁴⁺1	3

Puzzle #59

¹1	⁹⁺4	5	¹⁻2	3
⁹⁺4	5	⁷⁺3	⁴⁻1	³⁺2
⁸⁺3	²2	4	5	1
5	³⁺1	2	⁷⁺3	4
⁵⁺2	3	³⁻1	4	⁵5

Puzzle #60

⁹⁺5	4	³⁺1	2	³3
³⁺1	2	⁷⁺3	⁵5	⁵⁺4
²2	⁴⁻5	4	⁷⁺3	1
⁷⁺3	1	²2	4	³⁻5
4	³3	⁴⁻5	1	2

Puzzle #61

5+ 2	4+ 1	3	4− 5	6+ 4
3	13+ 4	5	1	2
9+ 5	3 3	4	5+ 2	4− 1
4	3+ 2	1	3	5
4− 1	5	9+ 2	4	3

Puzzle #62

9+ 5	4	10+ 2	8+ 3	1
5+ 2	3	5	4− 1	4
3− 4	4− 1	3	5	10+ 2
1	5	4 4	6+ 2	3
3 3	3+ 2	1	4	5

Puzzle #63

5× 5	1	2÷ 4	2	3× 3
4× 4	10× 5	2	15× 3	1
1	2÷ 2	15× 3	5	4 4
6× 3	4	5	2÷ 1	2
2	3× 3	1	20× 4	5

Puzzle #64

12× 1	2÷ 4	2	40× 5	15× 3
3	1 1	4	2	5
4	15× 5	3	2÷ 1	2
30× 5	2÷ 2	1	12× 3	4
2	3	20× 5	4	1

Puzzle #65

1 1	18× 3	2÷ 2	5× 5	20× 4
3	2	4	1	5
2÷ 2	25× 5	3 3	12× 4	2÷ 1
4	1	5	3	2
20× 5	4	2÷ 1	2	3 3

Puzzle #66

15× 3	1	2÷ 2	4	20× 5
5	15× 3	6× 1	2	4
2÷ 2	5	20× 4	3	3× 1
4	2÷ 2	5	1	3
1 1	4	30× 3	5	2

Puzzle #67

$^{6\times}$3	2	$^{4-}$5	1	$^{9+}$4
$^{4+}$1	3	$^{2\div}$4	^{2}2	5
$^{9+}$5	$^{3-}$4	2	$^{6\times}$3	1
4	1	$^{2-}$3	5	2
^{2}2	$^{4-}$5	1	$^{7+}$4	3

Puzzle #68

^{5}5	$^{6\times}$3	2	$^{9+}$4	1
$^{1-}$3	$^{4-}$5	1	^{2}2	4
4	$^{2\div}$2	$^{8+}$3	$^{4-}$1	5
$^{2\div}$1	4	5	$^{5+}$3	2
2	$^{3-}$1	4	$^{15\times}$5	3

Puzzle #69

$^{4+}$1	3	$^{4-}$5	$^{2\div}$4	2
$^{2\div}$2	4	1	$^{75\times}$5	3
^{3}3	$^{6+}$1	$^{2\div}$4	2	5
$^{11+}$4	5	$^{1-}$2	$^{4+}$3	1
5	2	3	$^{5+}$1	4

Puzzle #70

$^{12\times}$4	3	$^{8+}$5	2	1
$^{2\div}$1	$^{4-}$5	$^{1-}$3	$^{2\div}$4	2
2	1	4	$^{75\times}$3	5
$^{2-}$3	$^{2-}$2	$^{2\div}$1	5	^{4}4
5	4	2	$^{4+}$1	3

Puzzle #71

$^{4-}$1	$^{2-}$2	$^{10\times}$5	$^{12\times}$3	4
5	4	2	1	^{3}3
$^{3+}$2	1	^{3}3	$^{1-}$4	5
^{3}3	$^{20\times}$5	4	$^{10\times}$2	$^{2\div}$1
$^{12\times}$4	3	1	5	2

Puzzle #72

$^{2\div}$2	1	$^{2-}$3	$^{10\times}$5	$^{9+}$4
$^{3-}$4	^{3}3	1	2	5
1	$^{2\div}$2	$^{1-}$5	4	$^{4+}$3
^{5}5	4	$^{24\times}$2	3	1
$^{8+}$3	5	4	$^{2\div}$1	2

Puzzle #73

⁴⁻5	1	⁶ˣ2	3	²÷4
¹²ˣ4	3	⁹⁺5	⁴⁻1	2
³⁺1	²2	4	5	⁸⁺3
2	²⁰ˣ5	⁴⁺3	4	1
³3	4	1	³⁻2	5

Puzzle #74

¹⁻3	²÷1	2	¹⁰ˣ5	⁴4
4	⁵5	1	2	¹⁻3
⁴⁻1	²÷4	¹⁵ˣ5	⁷⁺3	2
5	2	3	4	⁶⁺1
¹⁻2	3	⁵⁺4	1	5

Puzzle #75

¹²ˣ4	¹⁰ˣ2	5	¹⁵ˣ3	1
3	⁹⁺4	²÷2	²÷1	5
²÷1	5	4	2	¹²⁺3
2	³3	²⁻1	5	4
⁴⁻5	1	3	²÷4	2

KenKen for all!

About the Author

Sophie currently is a high school junior in West Hartford, Connecticut. She loves solving KenKen puzzles, and she finished in the top 5 at the 2019 KenKen International Championship. Sophie has created a series of KenKen videos that are on her YouTube channel: KenKens with Sophie. The videos teach KenKen rules, vocabulary, and solving techniques. Sophie has designed and taught her KenKen curriculum to people of all ages, from elementary and middle school students to seniors in her community. She also serves as KenKen Puzzle, LLC's Social Media Manager, managing the official KenKen Puzzle Facebook and Instagram accounts to engage the KenKen community.

When not solving KenKen puzzles, you can find Sophie skiing with her sister, playing board games, reading a book, volunteering in her community or hanging out with friends.

Made in the USA
Las Vegas, NV
14 December 2021